It's true. The *real* Spanish no teacher dared to bring into the classroom is now at your fingertips:

¡AY, MIERDA! COJI EL TREN INCORRECTO.
(Oh, shit, I took the wrong train.)

ESTOY EN MARAVILLA QUE TODAVIA VIVO. ¡AY, DIOS, QUE NOCHE BRUTA!
(I'm amazed I'm still alive. Oh, God, what a bitchin' night!)

NO ME FRIEGAS!
(Don't jerk me around!)

SOSPECHO QUE TIENEN LOS DOS TODO EL TALENTO EN LA GLORIA.
(I think they both have all their brains in their genitals.)

¡CHINGATE!
(Go have sexual intercourse with yourself!)

And dozens more words, phrases, and mini-conversations for everything you always needed to say in Spanish—but nobody ever told you how!
¡MIERDA!

Frances de Talavera Berger has lived in Mexico, Spain, and Los Angeles, California—where she has never been at a loss for words.

¡MIERDA!

The Real Spanish You Were Never Taught in School

by
Frances de Talevera Berger

Illustrated by Michael Heath

A PLUME BOOK

PLUME
Published by the Penguin Group
Penguin Books USA Inc., 375 Hudson Street,
New York, New York 10014, U.S.A.
Penguin Books Ltd, 27 Wrights Lane,
London W8 5TZ, England
Penguin Books Australia Ltd, Ringwood,
Victoria, Australia
Penguin Books Canada Ltd, 10 Alcorn Avenue,
Toronto, Ontario, Canada M4V 3B2
Penguin Books (N.Z.) Ltd, 182-190 Wairau Road,
Auckland 10, New Zealand

Penguin Books Ltd, Registered Offices:
Harmondsworth, Middlesex, England

 REGISTERED TRADEMARK—MARCA REGISTRADA

ISBN-13: 978-0-452-26424-3
Printed in the United States of America
Set in Granjon
Designed by Nissa Knuth

Contents

¡MIERDA!

PREFACE

Castilian! The very sight of the word still gives you
fits, doesn't it? Remember the mind-boggling struggles
with that too inflexible, autocratic dialect which, for
obvious reasons, will always be the basis for teaching
Spanish? Sure, you've studied very hard and the pitfalls
of those lispy *cetas* and mystifying *tildes* have been hur-
dled. You feel you have a reasonable, functional command of Spanish. But do you? Think back a little.
Remember that Argentinian art film you could barely
understand? Or how about the latest East L.A. salsa
flick, supposedly in English but very heavy on Latino
slang? Might as well be listening to Martian, right?
Worse still, relive that mortifying moment on your first
trip to Mexico when, awestruck by the grandeur of the
world's largest pyramid, you gave vent to ecstasy in your
best scholarly Spanish—while two natives nearby stared
first at you, then at each other, and then politely but so
disdainfully rolled their eyes toward heaven!

Well, stop fretting. Basically, the problem is that your
Spanish is probably too prim, too proper, too formal for

just plain necessary communication. You weren't taught the colorful dirty words and fanciful phrases that are the heart and soul of this multiregional, dynamic language. Why, normal Hispanic usage practically *demands* heavy doses of superb *vulgarismo* (slang) and a heady repertoire of hard-core curses! Here, then, is an introductory guide to basic profanities without, however, any pretense toward the dogmatic or definitive. So hang in there—and you'll learn how everyday Spanish is *really* spoken, all the way from Pamplona to Tierra del Fuego.

Helpful Hints

Asterisks after words indicate a degree of dirtiness beyond the ordinary colloquial. A one-asterisk word may be used casually, but with moderation. As for the two-asterisk word, don't let it fill you with stark horror. Try it out, here and there. Play with it, cleverly. Go on, be brave. You'll soon find that the trick is to use it at just the right time *and* for just the right circumstance.

When not directly translatable, English definitions are given as close an equivalent as possible. But don't worry, the intent and flavor remain unspoiled.

An abbreviation will appear if a word or phrase is used mainly in the vernacular of a particular region or country: Spain = SPN; Mexico = MX; Puerto Rico = PR; East Los Angeles = ELA; Panama = PAN; Colombia = COL; Argentina = ARG; West Indies = W IND; Central America = C AMR; Cuba = CU. Also, since a majority of Hispanics concentrated in the American Northeast and Southwest are inventing a robust, ribald dialect of their own, *Spanglish* will be indicated as SPNGL when apropos.

¡MIERDA!

I
The Basics

Both Proper and Profane

Even the most common words have much juicier colloquial counterparts. Hispanics take great pride in applying as many words as possible to any and all objects—vegetable, mineral, and human. And if the language should fail to describe or impart one's exact meaning, there is no hesitation whatsoever to invent words, borrowing freely snips and pieces from other dialects and even from other languages. This isn't considered a bad habit. (Let the purists be damned!) On the contrary, it's applauded as imaginative and artistic. To a Latino, born with the compulsion of a poet, the most important thing in the world is to get his or her meaning across.

We begin with the proper—the lofty Castilian of the *hidalgos*—but then adjust quickly, of course, to the necessary and inventive profanities of the modern Hispanic tongue.

1

a man	un hombre
	un varón
	un macho (the best!)

| a guy | un tipo |
| | un tirante |

a friend	un amigo
	un compañero
	un pana (PR)

a true friend, a close buddy	un vero amigo
	un compadre (as close as a relative)
	un hermano (literally, a brother; or *mano*)
	un carnal** (but with affection, *obviously*)

a woman (still fecund)	una mujer
	una guapa (handsome— nice)
	una mamita* (in this case, not nice)
	una puta** (literally, a cunt or a whore)

a girl (nubile or not)	una muchacha
	una nena (SPN and MX)
	una chiquita
	una niña
	una baturra (SPN)

¡MIERDA!

a girlfriend	una **novia** una **amiguita** una **amante** (lover, but not always in the physical sense) una **tragona**** (*very* physical)
parents	**padres** **los viejos** (literally, old ones, but can be loving) **papi y mami** (very PR)
an old lady	una **anciana** (honored) una **bruja*** (a witch or hag)
a bastard	un **cabrón**** (sometimes in jest!) un **chi-chi cabrón**** (never jesting, very ELA)
a bitch	una **perra**** (like a female dog) una **puta**** (interchangeable with "cunt") **cuero**** (literally, a piece of leather)
son of a bitch	**hijo de puta****
a shit	**es mierda**** (as in *eres mierda* = you're shit)

a pig	un puerco* un cochino*
a male chauvinist pig	un machisto un macho cochino* un vero cabrón**
a fag (homosexually speaking)	maricón** gay (SPNGL—pronounced "guy") de la izquierda* (from the left side)

¡MIERDA!

picaflor** (MX = flower
snatcher)
mariposa** (MX =
butterfly)
pato** (PR = duck)
joto** (SPN)

a dyke (ditto, above)	lesbiana machua**
an ass licker	lambioso**

Likely Subjects to Be Roundly Cursed

the boss	el patrón el jefe el wise* (ELA—pro- nounced wees-ay; from "wise guy")
the landlord	el dueño el amo
the neighbor	el vecino el próximo (SPN)
the husband	el esposo el marido

the wife	la esposa la mujer la señora
the housewife	la ama de casa de condición humilde (literally, of humble station; a legacy of pure machismo!)
the mother-in-law	la suegra la bruja* (the witch—and often *quite* interchangeable)
the father-in-law	el suegro el padre lerdo* (MX = stupid)
the cabdriver	el taxista el cochero el simón (SPN—this will get you a cab *only* in Madrid) el cabby (SPNGL)
the clerk	el clérigo el esclavo* (literally, the slave—a real putdown)

the waiter	**el mozo** (in a café, bar, etc.) **el camarero** (for room service) **el bufete*** (or, like a walking veggy!)
what's-his-name, what's-her-name	**fulano(a) de tal** (SPN) **tal y fulano(a)** (MX—cute, right? But Spanish is like that, sometimes . . .)
you bunch of idiots	**bolla de idiotas** **pendejos*** (this gem will get all the explanation it *truly* deserves, later)
an all-around pain in the neck	**un fregado*** (this one also gets highlighted, later on!)
really, very	**de bien** **vero** **puro**

Everyday Necessities

a thing	**una cosa** **un objeto**
that thing	**tal cosa** **tal objeto**

poor thing!	**¡pobre!**
poor little thing!	**¡pobrecito(a)!**
a car	**un coche** **un carro** **un auto** **una máquina** ("machine"; used for almost any sort

of transport—except a
horse, of course)
una machín (MX and ELA)

a newspaper   **un periódico**
un papel (paper
un noticiero
un baratío (scandal sheet)
un mugrero* (porno)

a drugstore   **una droguería**
una farmacia
un medical (SPN)

a phone   **un teléfono**
una llama (MX—from
llamar, to call; a good
example of creative
speech!)
un fono (ELA)

a TV   **una televisión**
un teli
un tubo

a toilet   **un tocador** (can also mean
a chest of drawers, so be
careful)
un necesario
un retrete (for the very
polite)
un huicio (MX)

Frances de Talevera Berger

the police	la policía la guardia (SPN) la prole (MX) los tiros* (the shooters)
a whorehouse	una casa de idolatría (quite elegant!) una ramería** (quite *in*elegant) una casa libertina (quite Victorian ... and probably mundane) una chinchería** (literally, a bedbug house—and probably *not* boring)
a snack place (combining food, drinks, and coffee)	un cabaré (COL) un café un cafetín (slumming in MX) una cantina un milonguero (ARG = here, you might even be treated to a tango) un boiti (W IND influence in C AMR) una tapesa (SPN = cover—a spot serving *tapas*, those tiny, versatile snacks that *really* put a tight lid on hunger)

¡MIERDA!

Able-Bodied Adjectives

nice, friendly, warm, handsome (in short, anything good ...)	simpático
lousy, ugly, screwed-up, fucked (in short, anything bad ...)	piojoso infame chingado** manajado**
worthy	digno noble
useless	inepto vano fregado*
funny	cómico alegre chistoso nalgasón** (acting the asshole)

Vital Verbs

to understand	saber
not to understand a damned thing	saber ni una cosa condenada
to find	encontrar

11

to lose	**perder**
to be crazy about (to really like) something	**estar loco por**
to hate, to loathe	**odiar**
to bust some ass	**romper cola****
Go play with yourself!	**¡Manájate****!
Shove it up the ass!	**¡Pela las nalgas****!
Stick it up the cunt!	**¡Métetelo al funciete****!
Go fuck yourself!	**¡Chíngate****!
So there!	**¡A ver!**

Super Snippets

The following simply can't be uttered without involved body language! Oh, not the extroverted, extravagant variety, certainly, but the more *subtle* touches are definitely called for here. A shrug ... a sigh ... a slow lift of the eyes in understated but sincere supplication.... In Spanish, such gestures add profound dimensions if applied not with a sledgehammer, but with nuance and careful timing. Let's practice some indispensables along with foolproof moves.

¡MIERDA!

well	**pues**
(as in, *well*, I don't know)	

"Pues ... (*very, very slow shrug*) ... **no sé."**

Always pause for a long time after **pues**. Never rush. Think, reflect, gain time, decide, change your mind again, etc. With this one, the slower you go, the more respect you'll earn.

all right (OK)	**bueno**
(as in, *all right*, let's see)	**está bien**

"Bueno, vamos a ver ... (*small shrug*)."

The miniature move at the end defines the minimal amount of thought that silly problem probably deserves.

oh!	**¡ay!**

"A-a-a(*close your eyes for a split second*)**-y-y!"**

without a doubt!	**¡sin falta!**

"¡Ay! ¡Sin falta!"

If you mean it, say it crisply and toss your head back a fraction; if you don't, just tilt the head sideways a bit and take your time getting the sounds out.

so what?	**¿y qué?**

13

"¿Bueno ... (*lift the eyes, eloquently; shrug; set it up*) ... y qué?"

damn!	¡maldito!*
oh, my God!	¡ay, Dios mío! ¡Maldito
damn!	sea*!
	¡ay, Dios mío! ¡Condenado*!
by God!	¡por Dios!

"¡Condenado*! ¡No sé, por Dios!"

If you *really* don't know, say it with low-key fervor; however, don't waggle the arms around. That smacks of melodrama—and you may need that weapon later. If you're sincere, though, lift your hand (palm sideways) with a solid thrust upward. This is the most popular Latino gesture everywhere, and it's used to emphasize the highest moral values as well as the lowest, cheapest dirt!

Shut up!	¡Cállate!
	¡Cierra el hocico**! (MX = literally, shut your muzzle)
	¡Cállate la trompa*! (PR and CU = silence your horn)
	¡Clávate la mueca*! (SPN = nail your mouth shut)

Pronouncing, Pros and Cons

Don't get tongue-tied worrying that you might be mangling words. You're learning commonsense, everyday Spanish, after all! And keep in mind that each Hispanic subculture has produced its own rich variation of cadence and sound. Argentinians love to pop an English *j* in place of the first consonant of words (*yo* becomes *jo*, automatically). Puerto Ricans never bother ending their words; conversely, Cubans and Madrileños zoom from the beginning right to the end of a word, smugly swallowing all the vowels and consonants in the middle. Mexicans are meticulous pronouncers—and then they pin your ears back by lifting the voice at the end of each phrase, seeming always to be asking questions. And West Indians who have settled in Central America blithely ignore all accent marks and the like, singing out words as the spirit moves them! So speak out freestyle, practice your body moves, and don't forget to thrust the palm up and sideways.

Mini-Monologue

IT'S TIME TO TRY YOUR HAND AT SOME PRACTICAL SWEARING

1. Tal y fulano, tu amigo chistoso, me llamó.

2. Ese tipo es más que un amigo, es como un hermano.

3. ¿Tienes novia o esposa?

4. Tengo una mujer. Es muy simpática. ¡Dios mío, estoy loco por ella!

5. Pero mi suegra es una pura bruja. ¡También es mi vecina—y eso es chingado!

6. ¡Ay, cállate la trompa! Vamos a un cafetín a buscar unas mamitas.

7. ¡Hombre, no me friegues! A veces creo que no sabes ni una cosa condenada.

8. ¡Pues . . . y tú eres un vero cabrón!

1. What's-his-name, your funny friend, phoned me.

2. That guy is more than a friend, he's like a brother.

3. Do you have a girlfriend or a wife?

4. I have a wife. She's beautiful. My God, I'm crazy about her!

5. But my mother-in-law is a real witch. She's also my neighbor—and that's fucked!

6. Oh, shut up! Let's go to a café to look for hot chicks.

7. Man, don't screw around with me! Sometimes I think you don't know a damned thing.

8. Well ... and you're a real bastard!

II

The Many Ways of Dirty Self-Expression

First, That *Mierda* Word

Simply put, **mierda** means *shit*. It can bounce around as a noun, adjective, or verb. (But forget rules! You're about to become an innovator, right?) It appears in Spanish vernacular almost as often as it does in everyday English, but be warned that *mierda* is still considered a real shocker in most Hispanic circles. (Yes, that's true in Mexico as well, although *artful* swearing and cursing is considered a national sport.) Use the word in a restaurant, for instance, and a dish or two may crash to the floor. Fling it about casually in a cozy neighborhood *cantina*, even, and eyebrows will lift while glances are lowered—a superdramatic feat only Latinos have truly mastered. So use it sparingly, but when you do, make it count.

la mierda** = the shit (noun, but only if it really matters to you)

example: **¡Caí en pura mierda**!**
I fell in a pile of shit!

or: **¡Ay, mierditas**!**
Oh, (*literally*) little balls of shit!

¡Ay, mierda**!
Oh, shit!

and: **estar lleno(a) de mierda****
to be full of shit

also: **hacerlo como la mierda****
to do something all wrong

more
examples: **¡Eso es una mierda**!** (for a situation or for
an object)
That is shit!

¡Yo no soy una mierda**! (used mainly when
arguing with parents and/or lovers)
I am *not* shit!

Estoy metido(a) en pura mierda**.
I'm involved in a real shitty mess.

or: **Comí mierda**.**
I ate shit.
I didn't have a good time at that party, or
meeting, or at work, etc.

¡Come mierda**!
Eat shit!

also: un(a) comemierda (a snooty person—PR)

Other Vulgarisms

Like *mierda*, there are other words so vulgar, so loaded, but oh! so necessary for serious swearing that they also run amok in speech and trash every known grammatical rule. It's perfectly okay to rearrange them at will, and don't hesitate to drop them slam-bang into any part of a sentence. (Talk about using your imagination —this is it!)

cagar** = to crap

> **Tremenda cagada**!
> I *really* fucked up!

> **¡Lo cagué!**
> I ruined it!

> **¡Me cagué**!**
> I shit all over myself.

also: I really got scared.

> **Me hizo una cagada**.**
> He (she) did something very dirty to me.

joder** = (also) to fuck, to screw

¡No me jodas**!
Don't fuck around with me!

Me jodí**.
I fucked up.

Voy a joder** por ahí.
I'm going to fuck around (with women, or whatever—MX).

or: I'm going to go out and have fun (PR).
I'm going to do the town (sensually, of course).
I'm going to eat a lot, drink a lot, and fuck a lot!

carajo** = a very strong *hell*, or *damn* (mostly PR)

Vámonos pa'l carajo** antes de que venga la jara.
Hey, let's get the hell out of here before the cops come.

Me mandó pa'l carajo**.
He (she) sent me straight to hell.

¡Te voy a mandar pa'l carajo**!
I'm going to send you to hell!

¡Vete pa'l carajo**!
Go to hell!

¡MIERDA!

Metió la pata pa'l carajo.**
He (she) fucked up. (Literally, he (she) put the foot in it. Also = when a broad gets knocked up without the sanctity of marriage)

¡coño!* = a terrific "damn," or "the devil's ass"

¡Coño! ¡Qué bárbaro!**
Damn! What a jackass!

¿Qué coño te pasa?**
What the hell's the matter with you?

Es el coño, ese.**
That one is a devil.

ES EL COÑO**, ESE.

Frances de Talevera Berger

¿Cómo coño** lo quieres?
How the hell do you want it?

culo** = the ass (a truly X-rated *vulgarismo*)

tiene el culo** caliente
someone who is real horny

Me cayó como una patada en el culo**
He (she) struck me (figuratively) as a big
pain in the ass.

nada más sube el culo**
an easy lay

quebrar culo**
to bust ass

fregar* = to rub (the wrong way); to (literally) scour; to
annoy the hell out of somebody.

This one is a great favorite! It's not *too* dirty, but
add some graphic body language and you have a real
winner.

¡No me friegues*!
Don't jerk me around!

Está fregado*.
He's useless (or a pest, or rotten, or a pain in
the neck, or a screw-up, or *pues* ... get the
idea?).

24

¡MIERDA!

¡No hagas fregadas*!
Don't do stupid things!

Me fregó*.
He (she) did a rotten thing to me.

Me pasó una fregada*.
A lousy thing happened to me.

condenar* = to condemn strongly, to damn to hell

¡Esa condenada* me fregó* bien!
That goddamned woman did a real number
on me!

¡Condenado*! ¡No me quiebres el culo!**
Damn you! Don't bust my ass!

¡Esa casa condenada* me costó una mierda**
fortuna!**
That damned house cost me a shitty fortune!

¡Este condenado* calor me va a matar!
This goddamned heat is going to kill me!

pendejo* = a jerk, an idiot, a stupid fool, a total nerd (as
a noun)

Here is a rare colloquial gem! It can be stretched from
a noun into an adjective—even within the same sentence—
without fear of redundancy. For instance *Un pendejo*
*hace pendejadas*** = An idiot does stupid things. Simple,

25

right? But in Spanish, a truly florid language, nothing is ever that simple! You may call somebody a *pendejo** and mean it in a light, fond manner. Or you may mean it as one of the filthiest curses. It all depends on context, inflection, implication, sighs, groans, shrugs, the thrust of the hands (palms sideways, always!), the tilt of the head ...

example: **Mi compadre, Carlos, es un pendejo* raro.**
My buddy, Carlos, is an extraordinary person.

¡Qué pendejo* (*a sharp snap of the head*) **es ese Carlos!**
That Carlos is a super fuck-up!

¡MIERDA!

Sin duda, Carlos es pendejo*, pero también es macho bueno.
Without a doubt, Carlos is a nerd, but (he's) also a good man.

¡Carlos es puro pendejo*!
Carlos is a *total* bastard!

And the same goes for **pendejada(s)***. You may use it to describe the tiniest inconvenience—or a disaster of worldwide proportions.

example: **Qué pendejada* ... se me pasó el nombre de esa persona.**
What a stupid thing ... I forgot (it passed me by) that person's name.

¡Pendejo*! ¿Ya me vienes con *otra* pendejada*?

You stupid idiot! Are you coming to me with *another* fucking mistake? (You can see how useful this might be in the workplace, at school, etc.)

¡Vete! No me vengas con tus pendejadas*.
Go away! Don't come to me with your silly stories.

¡Si me haces una de tus pendejadas*, te voy a romper la cabeza condenada!
If you try one of your filthy tricks on me, I'll break your goddamned head!

Frances de Talevera Berger

Me quemé del sol, por pendejo(a)*.
I got sunburned because I was thoughtless.

**¡Ay, Dios mío—qué pendejada*! ¡Nos vamos
a morir todos! ¡Es un pendejo* temblor!**
Oh, my God—what a disaster! We're all
going to die! It's a fucking earthquake!

... uniquely Spanish, uniquely quixotic, *pendejo*!* Go
ahead and give it a try, grins and all. Tell a *pendejo** you
think he's done a *pendejada**. But be imaginative—and
be **careful.**

Mini-Monologue

Try These Sentences and See How Far You've Come

1. ¡Estás lleno(a) de mierda, pendejo(a)!

2. Coño, no me friegues. No más eres una pata en el culo.

3. Pues ... también estoy cansado(a) de tu caga.

4. ¡Si no cierras la trompa, condenado(a), te voy a dar una galleta!

5. Pobrecita, esa mujer está pendejada.

6. Bueno, voy a joder por ahí con una puta muy suave.

7. ¡Esos hébaros cagados (PR) me rompieron la ventana!

8. La vida es breve. ¡Vámonos pa'l carajo y vamos a joder toda la fregada noche!

¡MIERDA!

1. You're full of shit, you fucker!

2. Damn it, don't annoy me. You're just a pain in the ass.

3. Well ... I'm also fed up with (tired of) your crap.

4. If you don't shut your trap (your mouth), I'm going to slap your face!

5. Poor thing, that woman has a screw loose.

6. Okay, I'm going to screw around with a very classy bitch.

7. Those crappy youngsters broke my window!

8. Life is short. Let's go to hell with ourselves and drink and screw all goddamned night!

III
The Body

Functional and Graphic

Versatility is the rule of thumb here. Anybody can be just plain vulgar. But in Spanish, the goal is to be as colorful as possible. So the important thing is to keep your head as you navigate the colorful spectrum between the pristinely poetic and the more profoundly profane.... But then, when it's really time for the tough to get going, it's not only all right, but necessary, to get right down to it!

the body	**el cuerpo** **la figura** (SPN)
the head	**la cabeza** **la azotea** (PR) **la cáscara** (MX)
the face	**la cara** **la fach** (SPNGL)

LA CABEZA
LA AZOTEA (PR)
LA CÁSCARA (Mx)

LAS PARTES
LOS AGENTES**

what a mug!	¡qué cara!
the genitals	las partes
	los agentes**
the ass	el culo**
	el roto** (literally, crack or tear)

the buns	**el tracero*** (PR)
	las nalgas** (MX)
What hot buns (great buns)!	**¡Qué culo grande****!**
the breasts	**el busto**
	el pecho (also, chest)
the tits	**las tetas**
	los melones**
	los mangos**
	las mamas**
	los globos**
	las chupas** (includes nipples)
the pussy and cunt	**la cosita***
	la chocha** (MX and PR)
	el funciete (MX—and isn't it interesting that the definite article is masculine?)
	la crica**
the balls	**los huevos**** (MX)
	los cojones** (SPN)
	las bolas**
	los ping-pongs** (ELA—marvelous!)
the dick and cock	**el bicho**** (also, the name of a Cuban insect!)

> **el palo****
> **el pipí****
> **el pitón**** (literally, prong or point)
> **el todo**** (literally, *everything*; I mean, why mess around?)
> **el mentho**** (W IND influence in C AMR)

El mentho is a very interesting curse word. It can also mean "foul," among many other variations. It's used all over the Caribbean, Central America, and northwestern South America. One of the liveliest combos is *mentho* with *baile* = "dance." So for centuries (ever since indigenous West Indian languages melded with Spanish) the natives have been gloriously indulging in *dirty dancing*!

More Politely ...

There are times, of course, when off-color subjects come up even in the most polite company. It's great fun then to hear how the genteel manage to deal with gross. Some terribly charming examples are:

the whore

> **la puta**
> **la perdida** (the lost one)
> **la revoltosa** (wayward)
> **la caída** (the fallen one)
> **la tirada** (one who is tossed away; the same as the Italian *la traviata*)

¡MIERDA!

the genitals (male)	**el futuro**
	la gloria
	(No translation necessary for either of the above! But *machismo* is balanced, cynically, with . . .)
	el viejo (the old one)
	el enfermo (the sickly one)
	el flojo (the soft or lazy one)
	el absurdo (. . . but you've got the idea by now, surely)
the john, the toilet	**el baño** (bath)
damn!	**¡qué bárbaro!**
a prick teaser	**una chiflada**

A big fuss if often made of status: *de la primera* (first class) has very little to do with wealth, family ties, or position. A person or event may be tagged *de la segunda* (second rate) by whim, or gossip, or for the flimsiest reasons. All foreigners are *de la segunda*, of course, but Hispanics are even harsher on themselves and their own habits. And how they can laugh at their own foibles! And how clever, how euphemistic they can be when they say one thing—while really meaning something else entirely. The "status" method, with a double twist, can work this way:

35

Ese hombre ... no es de la primera.
(which may mean)
That man ... is not very important.

(or, on the other hand, if a woman is speaking to
    another)
That man ... (*a good, deep once-over*) is probably very
    boring in bed!

Esa señora tiene figura de la primera.
(which could mean)
That lady has a good figure.

(but if two men are speaking)
She's built like a brick shithouse!

Ese vestido es para segunderas.
(which is intended as)
That dress is ugly and unfashionable!

(but what she really thinks is)
Shit! I can't *afford* that damned dress!

Son nada más segunderas.
(preferably said with a nose-in-the-air *sniff*—for emphasis)
They're just a bunch of twats.

¡Ese político es honorable, sin falta!
(which on the surface seems to say)
That politician is honest, without a doubt!

(but, sarcastically, actually means)
That politician is a crook, believe me!

But even polite society eventually stops pussyfooting around. A great way to take the plunge and cut loose is to create lovely havoc by saying (in very contempo Spanglish), *"¡No estoy gufiando—te digo que te quiero fuquetear!"* You got that?

Mini-Monologue

It's Time to Sharpen Your Expertise

1. Tiene una facha muy bonita, María. ¿No crées?

2. ¡Sí, cómo no! Pero me gustan mejor las tetas de Alma. ¡Son maravillas!

3. Oyes, carnal, prefiero nalgas—y déjame decirte que María tiene un culo bien grande.

4. José es muy grosero. ¡Le gusta hablar cochinadas, pero imagino que es no más segundón!

5. Y su amigo Carlos es un chiflón. Friega como José.

6. Sospecho que tienen los dos todo el talento en la gloria.

7. ¡Tienes razón! No son simpáticos. Pero ya me cansé de hablar nada más de José y Carlos. Vámonos a la casa.

8. No, espérate. Todavía es temprano. Vamos a ver si José y Carlos son puros habladores. Quizás podemos enseñarles como se portan de los primeros.

9. ¡Ay, probrecita! ¿Qué les va a enseñar? ¡Es probable que son jotos condenados!

1. María has a very pretty face. Don't you agree?

2. Yes, and how! But I like Alma's tits better. They're marvelous!

3. Listen, buddy, I'm an ass man, myself—and let me tell you that María has great buns.

4. José is very vulgar. He likes to talk dirty, but I suspect (or imagine) he's boring in bed!

5. And his friend Carlos is just a tease. He's a pain in the neck, like José.

6. I suspect that both have all their brains in their genitals.

7. You're right! They're not too exciting. But I'm tired of talking only about José and Carlos. Let's go home.

8. No, wait. It's still early. Let's see if José and Carlos are really just full of hot air. Maybe we can teach them how to act like classy guys.

9. Oh, you poor thing! What are you going to teach them! They're probably goddamned fags!

IV
Sex, Everybody?

¡Cómo No!

Whether it's romantic, kinky, ordinary, or drop-dead stuff, sex talk in Spanish is always great fun! Learning a healthy repertoire of sweet nothings is a must, but you must also be aware of whose ear you are whispering into! There's a universe of difference between serious filth and the milder expressions attached to everyday matters of love and sex—so pay close attention and avoid the most embarrassing pitfalls.

to fuck, to screw	**chingar**** (the all-around, all-time traditional way to say "fuck")
	manajar**

A note of caution on the usage of *manajar*. It's the word most often misused by students because it's very much like the word *manejar*, which means to *drive*. You can imagine the hilarity (and bawdy rolling of the eyes) this mistake causes among the natives! So be sure you differentiate most clearly between your sexual impulse and your desire to rent a car....

fuquetear** (SPNGL— obviously an adaptation of "fuck" and now pretty widely in use)

chichar** (PR—"chichi" is a popular word for either male or female genitals. So *chichar* means the use of either one.)

meterlo** (literally, to stick it in)

to get laid   **acostarnos*** (to lie down together)

hacer el amor* (to make love poetically, romantically)

meter mano** (to stick the hand in)

meter palo** (to put the stick in)

rabiar** (ARG—literally, to rage together, to suffer together. For S & M athletes—an acquired taste)

to come   **venir****

comé** (SPNGL—pronounced "com-may")

¡MIERDA!

	el rapto supremo* (how lovely!)
	morir* (literally, to die = "to die in your arms")
	volar* (to fly, or explode)
blow job	**chupar**** (to suck)
	comer** (to eat)
	tragosas** (that which is swallowed)
69	**sesenta y nueve****
	al reverso** (literally, opposite)
to be in love	**estar enamorado(a)**
to be bewitched	**amor brujo**
one-sided love	**amor solo**
sad love	**amor lamento**
crazed love	**locura de amor**
lover	**amante**
to love with your whole being	**amar de corazón**
loved one	**querido(a)**

From Carnal Knowledge to Mother Love

Let's highlight a love word so versatile that it's known as an "iffy" word. (You'll get the idea as you go along, *sin falta.*)

querer   to love
to want
to wish
to yearn
to desire
to cherish
to like
to command
to resolve
to attempt

There are many more meanings, but now you've gotten the point! Interpretation is the key word here. Like English, you may say, "I love you" to your lover or your mother; unlike English, however, *te quiero* can run the gamut from "I love you, Mommy dearest" to "I want to fuck you, you bitch!" It makes all the difference in the world whether your interlocutor is your mother or sister—or somebody else's! In the case of the latter duo (in Hispanic circles), be very careful—at least at first.

Obviously, anything goes once a relationship gets intimate in a sexy sort of way (when in doubt, refer back to the first part of this chapter). But you are also urged to speak lyrical sweet talk to close family members (males included) to proclaim an entirely different sort of affection and appreciation. It's expected! And a whole vernac-

¡MIERDA!

ular of familial love talk has been cultivated for just this purpose. It's as extensive as the words and phrases for carnal love—and as unlimited as your imagination.

my soul	alma mía mi alma
my heart	mi corazón
little daughter (son) of my soul (or heart)	hijita(o) de mi alma (de mi corazón)
soul of my heart	alma de mi corazón
smile of my heart	sonrisa de mi corazón
warmth of my heart	calor de mi corazón
my life	vida mía mi vida
You are all my life	Eres toda mi vida
comfortable love	amor y compañía
like the love of God	como el amor de Dios
my love	amor mío mi amor
comfort of my heart	ensancho de mi corazón

You have my soul (heart) in your hands	**tienes mi alma (corazón) en tus manos**
You have no heart!	**¡No tienes corazón!**
I love you deeply	**Te llevo en el alma** (literally, I carry you in my soul)
I adore	**adoro**
I adore you	**te adoro**

¡MIERDA!

Of course, you're welcome to murmur any of the above to a lover, too. And it's a great compliment to call your true beloved *hermano* or *hermana* (knowing Latino culture by now, you figure out the reason why). As for Mother—unless the situation is very unorthodox—better leave her out of it.

Here's how to compliment *anybody:*

striking	**precioso(a)**
	tremendo(a)
	gracioso(a)
a handsome young person	**chulo(a)**
	lindo(a)
	adorable
handsome, good, friendly, nice	**muy simpático(a)**
	chévere (PR and COL)
	amable

Mini-Monologue

Exercises in the Carnal and Essential

1. ¡Estoy embrujada! Pienso en nada más que hacer el amor con él.

2. Imagino que es un amante tremendo y que sabe chichar como loco.

3. Lo quiero tanto y, pues ... soy capaz de todo con él, hasta chuparselo.

4. ¡Pero no a rabiar! Eso no me gusta. No lo hago ni con él.

5. Soñaré que nos acostamos y que voy a morir muchas veces.

6. ¡Pero lamento porque sé que nunca voy a manajarlo!

7. ¡Pues, sin embargo, puede ser que la fantasía es mejor que la vera chingadera!

1. I'm bewitched! I think of nothing but making love to him.

2. I imagine he's a marvelous lover and that he knows how to screw like crazy.

3. I love him so much and, well ... I would do anything with him, even sucking him off (or giving head).

4. But not S & M stuff! I'm not into that. I won't do that even with him.

5. I continually dream that we'll lie down together and I'll come many times.

6. But I'm sad because I know I'll never get to fuck him!

7. Well, it's possible that the fantasy is better than the actual fuck!

Mini-Monologue

Now Let's See How You Do With
Matters Maternal and Familial

1. Los nenes de Julia son la sonrisa de su corazón.

2. Los ama tanto que se pone triste cuando van a la escuela.

3. Y esos niños chulos adoran a su mamacita. La llaman "vida mía" y "mi corazón." ¡Qué lindos!

4. Es justo, porque Julia trata a *sus* padres con respéto y mucho amor.

5. ¿Sin embargo ... no piensas que todo eso paraguas es un poco abrumado? ¡A veces se me trastorna la panza!

6. Eso es porque los nenes tuyos no son muy amables. Les falta gracia.

7. ¡Y los tuyos, querida, se portan como segunderos de la calle! ¡Adiós, hermanita de mi alma!

1. Julia's children are the smile of her heart.

2. She loves them so much that she can't bear to see them go off to school.

3. And those pretty children adore their mother. They call her "my life" and "my heart." They're so sweet!

4. That's as it should be, because Julia treats her parents with respect and lots of love.

5. Still ... don't you think all that mush is a little overdone? Sometimes it turns my stomach!

6. That's because *your* children are not very nice. They are ill-mannered.

7. And yours, my dear, act like low-life little beggars! Good-bye, little sister of my soul!

V
Filthy Flights of Fancy

Or, How to Get Even with
Your Car, Spanish Style

Latins wholeheartedly believe (or, so they would have everybody else believe) that inanimate objects have reasoning powers. They kiss favorite pictures, and they kick chairs that always seem to be in the way. Not that objects have souls (blasphemy!), but they're convinced that inanimate things have urges, good and bad, just like humans. When bought, objects are blessed with holy water; if loved (tables, houses, taco stands, lawn mowers, and especially cars, to name a very few), they are often awarded pet names. And then there are those inanimate things that are capable of varying degrees of sheer nastiness. If discarded because of "bad temper"—often still new—those things are thoroughly cursed straight to hell! Oh, yes, they talk to furniture, or whatever, as they will to either angelic or demonic half-wits. This isn't crazy, you know, this is just Spanish. And what a delightful and fanciful way to sublimate secret love, or to get rid of rage and frustration without hurting anybody.

example: (remember, the owner is never at fault) **¡Ese pendejo martillo se me saltó de la fregada mano y se plantó—¡chinga!—en el pie!**

(That stupid hammer jumped out of my goddamned hand and plunked itself down— fuck!—on my foot!)

¡MIERDA!

or: (if the owner wishes to be even more gorgeously creative) **¡Esa puta Carmen se desinfló la llanta cabrona otra vez!**

(That bitchin' Carmen [a car, not a woman] let the air escape out of its bastard tire again!)

or: (becoming even more fanciful and melodramatic) **¡Ay, coño! Esa puta Carmen se desinfló la fregada llanta cabrona otra maldita vez— ¡por el amor de Dios!**

(Oh, shit! That cunt Carmen let the fucking air escape out of its bastard tire one more damned time—for the love of God!)

and: **¡Ese ropero se le metió el demonio! Está chingado. Siempre me pega en la canilla. ¡Lo voy hacer pedazos!**

(That wardrobe is full of the devil! It's fucked. It always hits me on the shin. I'm going to tear it to pieces!)

also: **Yo no sé que le pasó al pendejo teli. A veces trabaja, y a veces no. ¡Hace lo que le da la chingada gana! ¡Le hablé, muy amable, pero me sigue haciendo burla, como cagado!**

(I don't know what's happened to that stupid TV. Sometimes it works and sometimes it doesn't. It does what it fucking well pleases!

55

I spoke to it, very nicely, but it's still playing
its shitty tricks on me!)

How to Completely Fuck Up Your Pet

The love of animals is something very basic in Hispanic
culture. Almost every household has its pet or two or
three—and the poor little darlings are very nearly loved
to death. Oh, how they're pampered! Even in this day of
nutritiously balanced commercial pet foods, great pains
are taken to cook up special saucy tidbits for beloved
beasties—treats so rich, so loaded with spices that it's a
wonder spleens don't splatter within six months! Even
farm animals become actual family members. You'll hear
no Spanish derivatives of "Fido" or "Skippy" or "Whiskers"
—and that's because most pets are given proper *human*
names. Classical names are favored, so you'll have no
trouble finding jewels such as Mosé the goat, Hector the
Great Dane, Desdemona the cat, Dalila the goldfish, and
Matamoros† the horse! And pets are always included in
familial love talk, so don't forget to say (whispering)
vida mía and (nuzzling) *calor de mi corazón* and (kissing
on the nose) *¡te adoro!* when talking to the animals.

†The honorific conferred on one of Spain's greatest generals, who destroyed so
many of the enemy that he's known as "Killer of Moors."

¡MIERDA!

Standard Household Variety

dog	**perro(a)**
puppy	**perrito(a)**
little dog	**perrillo(a)**
lap dog	**perrillo(a) de falda**
cat	**gato(a)**
kitten	**gatito(a)**
bird	**pájaro**
	ave
canary	**canario**
parrot	**papagayo**
	loro (COL)
parakeet	**periquito**
white mouse	**ratón blanco**
small snake	**culebra chica**

Common Barnyard Animals

rabbit	**conejo**
donkey	**burro**
horse	**caballo**
goat	**cabra**
	chivo
chicken	**gallina**

Frances de Talevera Berger

Mini-Monologue

It's Time to Review
Vulgarismo—ELA and Spanglish Style!

1. Conozco una guapa que no es puta ni chiflada.

2. ¡Coño, pero su hermano sí es un verdadero chi-chi cabrón! ¡Le presté mi carro, y la puta pendejo lo machicó y me lo entregó en pedacitos de mierda!

3. Mientras, ojalá que encuentro pronto un huicio. Tengo que mear como el demonio.

4. Parece que esa pobre bruja perdió algo. Pero, caga, no hay tiempo para ayudarla porque voy a encontrar mi amigo, un puro carnal, y vamos a pasar el tiempo.

5. Tal vez cruzamos el barrio en mi carro. ¡Chingado—se me olvidó que no tengo coche! El cochino está machado. ¡Pues, quizás en vez vamos a buscar un parti bien rico donde se puede mover las colas en ritmo con mamitas de nalgas chulas!

1. I know a good-looking woman who isn't a bitch or a prick teaser.

2. Damn it, but her brother is a real bastard. I loaned him my car, and the son-of-a-bitch jerk smashed it up and returned it to me in shitty little pieces!

3. Meanwhile, I hope I find a toilet fast. I have to piss like the devil (like crazy).

4. It looks as if that poor old hag has lost something. But, crap, there's no time to help her because I'm

¡MIERDA!

meeting a friend, a true buddy, and we're going to hang out.

5. Maybe we'll cruise the neighborhood in my car. Fuck—I forgot the shitty thing is smashed up! Well, perhaps we'll look for a real happening party where we can dance (move our asses) to the beat (in rhythm) with some foxy women (literally, big tits and cute buns).

VI
No, I Am Not a Turista!

Or, Where the Holy Hell Am I?

¡ ... pícaros, putas, pleytos, polvos, piedras, puercos, perros, piojos, y pulgas!

(... rogues, whores, fights, dust, stones, swine, dogs, lice, and fleas!)

> A Dutch tourist's observations on sixteenth-century Valladolid, then the capital of Spain

Hispanics rarely give straight directions indicating east, west, north, or south. Maybe that's because they love sending visitors on meandering tours past beloved local sites, whether those are renowned masterpieces in major capitals or dubious rock piles in backwater villages. You will probably be told, "The post office? Of course! Keep going until you reach the plaza. (You can't miss it! It's so big! So important!) There, stop at the Café Goya. (Rest! Have a cool drink! Eat a morsel or two of the best food in town!) Then leave the plaza by way of the Fountain of the Archangels. (Oh, it's so beautiful!) Turn left after you pass through the Gate of Iron, and then go along the Street of Innocent Children until you come to our cathedral. (Go inside, please! Feast your eyes on the exquisite artwork!) ..."

Well, eventually you may get to the post office; perhaps, with luck, you've also seen some wonders not on your itinerary. Here are some necessities for the traveler (yes, even ordinary, commonsense words and phrases— and all can be topped off with crafty curses).

to the left	**a la izquierda**
to the right	**a la derecha**
straight ahead	**derecho**
east	**este**
	oriente
west	**oeste**
	occidente
north	**norte**
	septetrional
south	**sur**
	meridional
Where is ... ?	**¿Dónde es ... ?**
	¿Dónde está ... ?

¡MIERDA!

Please, how do I get to . . . ?	¿Cómo llego a . . . por favor?
How do I find . . . ?	¿Cómo encuentro . . . ?
What are the hours at . . . ?	Cuáles son las horas de . . . ?
Help me! I'm lost.	¡Ayúdame! Estoy perdido(a).
Oh, shit! I took the wrong train.	¡Ay, mierda**! Cojí el tren incorrecto.
I'm wrong—I know.	No tengo razón—lo sé.

¡AY, MIERDA**! COJÍ EL TREN INCORRECTO

What time does the mail arrive?	¿A qué hora llega el postal?
Where do I find a post office?	¿Dónde encuentro un correo?
Where is the Museum of Fine Arts?	¿Por dónde está el Museo de Bellas Artes?
Like a damned fool, I went down the *other* street!	¡Pasé por la *otra* calle, por pendejo*!
Goddamn it! I should have taken the *first* turn.	¡Coño**! Debería haber cogido la *primera* gira.
to turn back	volver atrás
to turn down	boca abajo (also, upside down)
money	moneda dinero sueldo
Where can I exchange money?	¿Dónde se cambia dinero?
bank	casa de banco banco
black market	tráfico mancho (literally, stained traffic)

¡MIERDA!

sueldo abajo (literally,
money from below)

hotel

hotel
posada

boardinghouse

casa de huéspedes
pensión

police station

comisaría de policía

Where the hell can I find
a cop?

¿Dónde puedo encontrar
un guarda, por el
demonio*?

I lost my camera, for God's
sake!

¡Perdí mi cámara, por el
amor de Dios!

Oh, hell—*I'm* the one
who's lost!

¡Maldito*—yo soy el que
estoy perdido!

to take a nap

echar un siesta (literally, to
throw oneself into a
short sleep)

I'm hungry!

¡Tengo hambre!

to dress

vestir

to go out on the town

ir por ahí

Frances de Talevera Berger

From the Night Before to the Morning After

And as you "do the town," you're sure to meet interesting people and have yourself a fabulous time:

to have a bite (eat lightly)	**meriendar**
to eat a lot	**comer como lobo** (literally, to eat like a wolf) **hacerse puerco** (to turn into a pig)
to have a small appetite	**ser de boca chiquita** (literally, of the small mouth!)
soup	**caldo** **sopa**
potato	**papa** **patata**
sweet potato	**batata** **camote**
vegetable	**vegetal** **legumbre**
vegetarian	**vegetariano** **fitófago**

66

¡MIERDA!

meat	**carne** **vianda**

(The different ways meat can be cooked and served are: chopped, *picadillo*; cold, *fiambre, fría*; stewed, *cocido, estofado*; roasted, *asada*; sautéed, *guisada*; barbecued, *a la parrilla*.)

salad	**ensalada**
dessert	**postre** **dulce**
red wine	**(vino) tinto**
white wine	**(vino) blanco**
This wine is sour!	**¡Este vino está agrio!**
This food stinks!	**¡Esta comida apesta!**
This food is great!	**¡Esta comida es muy buena!**
The check, please.	**La cuenta, por favor.**
to take a stroll	**pasearse** **al paseo**
the mayor (of a city)	**el alcalde**
a very famous person	**una persona muy famosa**

tramp, or bum	**vago** **sinvergüenza** (literally, one without shame)
pimp	**chulo** **alcahuete** (SPN) **bimbo*** (ELA—yes, the same as the hooker) **cilaso**** (PAN)

ARREBATAR **
VOLAR
PONERSE EN ALGO CHINGADO **

¡MIERDA!

drug addict	**tecato** (PR)
	marijuano (MX)
	adicto
	entregado (literally, to be given to drugs)
	craqueado (SPNGL)
to get high	**arrebatar****
	volar
	ponerse en algo chingado**
to really get fucked up	**chicaíto****
	embarrado (literally, smeared)
	troncado (literally, cut off— from reality)
	trompado* (ELA = having a snootful)
marijuana, weed, grass	**yerba**
	pasto
	mote
	material
	la cuca

The arguments over the origin of the word *marijuana* are endless. The one that seems to make the most sense is: *mari'*, from *mariada(o)* = "dizzy"; *juana*, from *Juana* = in Spanish, the same as "Jane Doe" or "Every-woman." So we have (I kid you not) "a plant that makes everybody dizzy." *Mierda—no me digas!*

69

a drunk	**un borracho(a)**
to get drunk	**emborracharse**
drunk as a fucking skunk	**borracho(a) como un chingado** zorillo**
Oh, my God, my stomach hurts!	**¡Ay, Dios mío, me duele la barriga!**
Shit—my head is splitting!	**¡Mierda**—me mata la cabeza!** (literally, my head is killing me!)

Mini-Monologue

The Morning After ...

1. Me maravillo que todavía estoy vivo. ¡Ay, Dios, que noche bruta!

2. Me chingé tanto que no recuerdo donde dejé mi fregada cámara. Iré a la policía para dar noticia que la perdí cuando me calma mi barriga.

3. Me gustó mucho el restaurante donde fuimos. La comida salió muy buena—mucho mejor que esa suciedad que nos dan en nuestra pensión, sin duda.

4. Sí, pero gritaste como perro loco cuando nos dieron la cuenta!

5. ¿Y, por qué nó? Esa carne asada nos costó una fortuna. Y la botella de tinto también.

¡MIERDA!

6. ¡Pero gozamos—así, por qué fregar? ¿Dime, como acabamos hablando con un vago? ¡Qué cochino!

7. ¡Qué pendejo eres, hombre! Él no es un vago. ¡Él es el alcalde de la ciudad!

8. ¡Mierda! ¡Lo que necesito es una pica de la cuca!

1. I'm amazed that I'm still alive. Oh, God, what a bitchin' night!

2. I got so fucked up that I don't remember where I left my stupid camera. I'll go to the police to report that I lost it as soon as my stomach calms down.

3. I really liked that restaurant we went to. The food turned out great—so much better than the garbage they give us at our hotel, without a doubt.

4. Yes, but you howled like a mad dog when they gave us the bill!

5. And why not? That roast beef cost a fortune. And the bottle of red wine too.

6. But we enjoyed ourselves—so why bitch? Tell me, how did we wind up talking to a bum? What a pig!

7. Man, you're really a nerd! He's no bum. He's the mayor of the city!

8. Shit! What I need is a puff on a joint!

VII
The Graces

Or, How to Turn Good Clean Fun into Devilish Dirt

Fiesta has become an international word for "party," and no culture enjoys a good time more than Latinos. Any excuse will do for music, singing, and dancing. The roots of this joyous *ambiente* (atmosphere) go back to the Persians and the Moors and ancient Iberia. As Spanish influence spread to the New World and the Pacific, so did the idea of endless, wonderful celebration.

a celebration

una fiesta
una celebración
una festividad
un festejo

to enjoy

gozar
disfrutar
saborear

music	**música**
to sing and dance	**cantar y bailar**
to drink	**beber** **tomar**
A toast!	**¡Un brindis!** **¡A la salud de ...!** **¡Salud, dinero, y amor!** (literally, health, wealth, and love)
a party that's a drag; a date who won't screw	**pura música, pero nada de ópera** (literally, lots of music, but no opera!)
a fancy-dress ball	**un baile de trajes**
a masked ball	**un baile de máscaras**
a variety show	**unas variedades**
a drag show (as in "gay")	**una escena de patos****
a porno show	**una escena chingo****
a porno film	**un flic chi**** (ELA) **película desgraciada*** **cine negro**
a funny movie	**una película cómica**

¡MIERDA!

a birthday party · una fiesta de cumpleaños

an anniversary celebration · un festejo de aniversario

a celebration on a farm, or in the countryside · una fiesta ranchera

a barbecue · un asado al aire (literally, cooked in the open air)

a picnic · una jira en el campo
una romería (like the Romish, or Gypsies)

a folk song · una canción popular
un romance
una copla

a folk dance · un baile típico

to dance in rhythm · bailar a compás

so happy · ¡qué alegre!

This is boring! · ¡Qué pesado! (literally, too heavy to bear)

Let's shove off! · ¡Vamos a matar chinches a otras partes! (literally, let's go kill bedbugs somewhere else!)

Hurry up!	¡A prisa!
Let's get the hell out of here!	¡Vámonos como el demonio!

Just Hanging Out and Shooting the *Mierda!*

Another favorite pastime is sitting or standing around talking. Hispanics just love to bullshit, and subjects range from the sublime to the very base, often in the same conversation! A great example of filthy wit is found in *coplas* (either sung or spoken). Call them proverbs or sayings; whatever the name, this type of art form is usually cutting—and always quite entertaining.

El hombre sabe que hacer con la vida desde que sabe que hacer con su propia mierda**.
(Man learns how to deal with *life* once he learns how to cope with his own *shit*.)

Camarón que se duerme, se lo lleva la corriente. (Literally: When a shrimp falls asleep, then the current will carry him away. Loosely: If you don't stay alert, you'll fuck up.)

A caballo regalado no se le mira el colmillo.
(Never look a gift horse in the mouth.)

La cotorra que chi, no canta.
(Literally: While the parrot pisses, it doesn't sing. Loosely:

¡MIERDA!

You can't do two things at the same time and do them right.)

¡Me lo metió mongo**!
(Literally: He shafted me with a soft prick. Loosely: He *really* made a fool of me!)

Ni chiche**, ni limonada.
(Literally: He (she) doesn't fuck, or drink lemonade. Loosely: He (she) does neither this nor that. Or: That person does *nothing*.)

No le busques cinco patas al fregado* gato.
(Literally: Don't be looking for five paws on the shitty cat. Loosely: Don't go out of your way to look for trouble.)

Él que se acuesta con perros, con pulgas se levanta.
(He who sleeps with dogs wakes up with fleas.)

Él que arqueda la botella no arqueda la mujer.
(He who strokes a bottle does not fuck a woman.)

Reniego de bestia que en invierno tiene siesta.
(Literally: I disown any animal who sleeps all winter. Loosely: I'll have nothing to do with a lazy person.)

¡La que se tira como tapete suplica las patadas!
(She who throws herself on the floor like a rug begs to have people wipe their feet on her!)

77

¡Si lo manajas, no te lo metas en la boca!**
(If you fuck it, don't stick it in your mouth! Or, Don't
eat what you've already fucked!)

VIII
Sorry, It's *Really Big* Test Time!

Oh, come on, you've come this far—don't skip the grand finale! It's actually quite painless. Familiar colloquialisms will be mixed up like crazy in the paragraphs below, so gird your loins (use your head, too) and take a healthy whack at identifying the literary and historical folks described. The answers appear on another page, but no damned peeking, okay? Why, *comemierda*, you'll at least recognize the curse words, won't you? So relax, get ready, and have some fun—*y buena suerte, amigos!*

1. Como vero pendejo, el viejo trastornado manejó su pobre caballo rapidamente pa'dar guerra contra molinos de pura fantasía. "¡Mierda!" gritó el viejo, "les voy a cortar los cojones!" Los molinos no hicieron caso, por cierto. Revoltijado y fregado, el viejo lamentó a su compadre (¡el de la panza tremenda!), "¡Vámonos de aquí— vámonos por ahí a buscar puta!" Tal, los dos amigos llegaron a un pueblo miserable. Encontraron una chiflada chula con globos lindos y nalgas de maravilla. "Te voy hacer una gran señora," le dijo, en rapto, el viejo menso. "¡Vete al demonio, hombre!" respondió la puta.

Frances de Talevera Berger

"Lo que quiero es *comida.* ¡Tengo hambre!" Pero el pobre viejo no tenía nada de dinero. "¡Entonces," le dijo la chiflada, "voy sin comer, y tú, que vayas con Dios—*y sin nada de chocha!*"

2. "¡Levanta el culo, condenado, y ayúdame derrotar los Moros desgraciados!" la reina renegó al rey. "Tú te quedas aquí, en el castillo, chingando niñas preciosas—y yo soy la que tengo que pelear como un fuquete macho!" El rey flojo respondió, "¡Por el amor de Dios, mujer, déjame en paz!" La reina se puso furiosa. "Está bien, cabrón. Disfruta. ¡Entonces, *yo* hago lo que me dé la gana!" Y unos dicen que la reina dejó el rey con su paz, y que ella hizo lo natural con un marinero Italiano un poco tocadito. ¡El pobrecito pensó que el mundo era redondo! ¡Pues ... quién sabe ...?

3. "¡Ay, Dios mío, ya no puedo joder más! ¡Imagínate! ¡Ya metí el palo en mil putas, en España, solo! ¡Ya me cansé de ser el amante tremendo! Coño, me duelen los ping-pongs. ¡Y el chiste es, que me gustan mejor los baturros suaves! Dame mi vestido de baile. ¡Bastante mierda! ¿Donde encuentro cerca una cantina de jotos?"

And then there's another worthy character who deserves recognition:

4. "¡Qué alegría! ¡Puedo entenderlo casi *todo!*"

The Answers

But *You* Don't Need Them ...

1. Like a true fool, the mad old man rode his poor horse quickly to do battle against windmills of pure fantasy. "Shit!" yelled the old man. "I'm going to cut your balls off!" The windmills ignored him, of course. Messed up and fucked over, he lamented to his friend (the one with the great big belly), "Let's get out of here—let's go around and find some hot pussy!" So the two friends arrived at a miserable little village. There they met a pretty prick teaser who had lovely tits and a marvelous ass. "I'm going to turn you into a great lady," the stupid old man ecstatically told the whore. "Man, go to hell!" said the cunt. "What I really want is *food.* I'm hungry!" But the poor old man had no money. "In that case," responded the prick teaser, "I'll go without eating, and you can go with God—*and without any pussy!*"

2. "Get off your ass, God damn you, and help me defeat those disgusting Moors!" the queen swore at the king. "All you do is stay here, in the castle, pronging pretty little girls—and I'm the one who has to fight like a fucking jock!" The lazy king retorted, "For the love of God, wife, leave me in peace!" The queen was furious. "Okay, you bastard. Enjoy yourself. Then I'll do whatever the hell *I* want!" And some say that the queen left the king to his peace, and that she did her thing with an Italian sailor who had a few screws loose. He thought the world was round! But ... who knows ...?

3. "Oh, my God, I can't fuck anymore! Think of it! I've stuck my prick in a thousand cunts, in Spain alone! I'm tired of being the great lover! Fuck, my balls hurt. And the joke is that I much prefer soft young boys! Give me my ball gown. I've had enough of this shit! Where can I find the nearest gay bar?"

4. "What happiness! I can understand almost *everything!*"

Frances de Talevera Berger

1. Don Quixote
2. Queen Isabella
3. Don Juan
4. *You!*